John Thomas Porter

Elements of Brakigraphy

A system of phonic shorthand writing, founded upon the vowel sounds of

the English language

John Thomas Porter

Elements of Brakigraphy
A system of phonic shorthand writing, founded upon the vowel sounds of the English language

ISBN/EAN: 9783337085025

Printed in Europe, USA, Canada, Australia, Japan

Cover: Foto ©Paul-Georg Meister /pixelio.de

More available books at **www.hansebooks.com**

ELEMENTS

OF

BRAKIGRAPHY:

A SYSTEM OF

PHONIC SHORT-HAND WRITING,

FOUNDED UPON THE VOWEL SOUNDS OF THE
ENGLISH LANGUAGE.

ADAPTED FOR SELF-INSTRUCTION,

AND USE IN SCHOOLS AND ACADEMIES

BY

JOHN T. PORTER,

STENOGRAPHER.

PITTSBURGH:
PRINTED BY JOS. EICHBAUM & CO.
1883.

PREFACE.

THIS little volume is intended to answer a two-fold purpose —as a manual for self-instruction, and as a text-book for use in the school room. The lessons are so graded and arranged that, with three or four hours' practice per day, the principles may be mastered in a month. The thousands of arbitrary symbols called word-signs, which constitute the bulk of the writing in the old systems of short-hand, and which prevent those systems from being reduced to a science, are avoided in Brakigraphy. The student pursues the study as a science, and having mastered the principles, a few months spent in the practical application of them will enable him to record the exact words of the most rapid speaker.

We live in an age of improvement. The growing needs of humanity are being constantly supplied by the wonderful discoveries and inventions of science. To keep pace with the flurry and rush of business, a speedier method of writing is demanded, and within four or five years the attention of the business world has been directed towards short-hand as a means of relief from the drudgery of the common writing. The relief thus afforded has only been partial, from the fact that the old systems of short-hand in use are so unscientific and arbitrary in their character that but comparatively few persons ever acquire a competent knowledge of them; and even when acquired, the writing is practically a sealed book to all but the writer himself.

Having had an uninterrupted practice of thirteen years as a Law Reporter in the Courts of Pennsylvania, I may be presumed to have some knowledge of the requirements of a system of short-hand destined to become a universal medium through which business may be transacted. Such a system must possess certain requisites, the most important of which are: simplicity of construction, so that it may be learned in a few months by persons of ordinary ability; that it be equal to speech in speed; and that it be easily read, not only by the writer himself, but by others familiar with the same system. In the development of Brakigraphy, it has been my aim to perfect such a system of short-hand. How well I have succeeded I leave the public to judge.

The average rate of public speaking is estimated to be about one hundred and twenty words per minute. In the class-room, I have trained students in six months to write one hundred and fifty words per minute from dictation, and to read their short-hand notes almost as readily as the common writing, although entirely unfamiliar with the subject-matter.

It is believed that this is the first time the art of short-hand writing has been presented to the public in a scientific form; and the favorable reception Brakigraphy has already met with at the hands of the public, encourages me to believe that the present edition, after the careful revision I have given it, will meet with still greater favor.

CONTENTS.

BRAKIGRAPHY.

DIRECTIONS TO THE STUDENT.

The first chapter contains the theory upon which Brakigraphy is founded, and should be thoroughly mastered. Three or four hours a day for a week may be devoted to it profitably.

Each line should be learned separately until the phonics can be pronounced aloud and written at the same time, without the aid of the book.

When the theory is understood the first reading exercise should be taken up, and first read over carefully with the aid of the translation, and finally written over and over until it can be written correctly from dictation.

The first chapter thus learned, the second will be found much easier, but the practice on it should not be omitted until the reading exercise can be written correctly from dictation.

Beginners are generally ambitious to advance rapidly, forgetting the fact that learning to write well is the most important. This can be accomplished best by taking special pains with the first chapter, the characters of which are arranged in groups for the purpose of disciplining the memory and the pen of the writer.

While learning the first ten chapters, do not try to write rapidly, but well. The eleventh chapter, however, should be written over and over until a speed of one hundred words per minute is attained.

Always use pen and ink in practice. The best reporters hold the pen between the first and the second finger, as in back-hand writing.

If these directions in regard to the first two chapters are faithfully carried out, the student will find his future practice pleasant and easy; but to insure rapid progress the remaining chapters of the principles should be learned with the same thoroughness as the first two.

CHAPTER I.

SECTION I.

In order to obtain a clear understanding of the **correct** sounds of the phonic vowels, **it is** necessary for the student **to** know **the meaning of the diacritical points used in the** English orthography to indicate the peculiar **sounds of the** English vowels, thus:

LONG VOWELS.   SHORT VOWELS.

ē, as in eat,   ĭ, as in hit,

ā,   "   ate,   ĕ,   "   met,

ä,   "   ,arm,   ă,   "   hat,

ô,   "   odd,   ŭ,   "   hut.

ō,   "   ode,

oo   "   mood.

DIPHTHONGS.

ī, as in ire,

oi, "   oil,

ou, "   out.

Repeat the **sounds of the** pointed vowels as found **in the** following words, until **the** correct sound of **each can be given** readily and accurately:

e-at, a-te, a-rm, o-dd, o-de, m-oo-d, **h-i-t, m-e-t,** h-a-t, h-u-t,

ē,   ā,   ä,   ô,   ō,   oo,   ĭ,   ĕ,   ă,   ŭ,

i-re, oi-l, ou-t.

ī,   oi,   ou.

FIRST GROUP.

Brakigraphy is founded upon thirteen vowel sounds, **which** are represented **by the** thirteen pointed letters above.

Each one of these pointed vowels is represented by a short-hand character called a phonic, thus :

1. ē,   ā,   ä,   ô,   ŏ,   oo,   ĭ,   ĕ,   ă,   ŭ,   ĩ,   oi,   ou.

The long vowels and the diphthongs **oi** and **ou** are repre-sented by long phonics, the short vowels and the diphthong **i** are represented by short phonics.

Each phonic takes its sound from its position with **reference to the line of** writing, as above, on, below, or through **the line.**

In the second line the phonics are **written from left to right, inclining** obliquely downward, which indicates **that the con-sonant** *r* is combined with the vowel, thus:

2. ēre, āir, är, ôr, ôre, oor, ĭr, ĕr, är, ŭr, īre, oir, our.

In the third line the phonics are **written** from right to **left inclining** obliquely downward, which indicates that the **con-sonant** *l* is combined with the vowel, thus:

3. ēle, āle, äl, ôl, ôle, ool, ĭl, ĕl, äl, ŭl, īle, oil, oul.

Practice on the first group until the phonic characters representing the following words can be written from memory in their proper positions with reference to the line of writing :

PRACTICAL EXERCISE.

awe, owe, ah, eye, ear, air, or, oar, ire, our, err, eel, ale,

all, ill, ell, oil, owl.

SECTION II.

SECOND GROUP.

The three lines composing the first group form the basis upon which the subsequent structure is to be erected, and the student having mastered them, is now prepared to advance a step.

The second group is similar to the first, except that the phonics are made a little longer, and curved, which indicates that the consonant *m* is added to the vowels and the combinations.

Beginners generally experience some difficulty in noting the difference between the first three phonics and the second three in the second and the third line below. This difficulty is easily overcome by practice, and will vanish entirely by the time the student has reached Chapter III.

All oblique phonics should be written with a downward movement of the pen.

1. ĕme, ăme, ăm, ŏm, ŏme, oom, ĭm, ĕm, ăm, ŭm, ĭme, oĭm, oum.

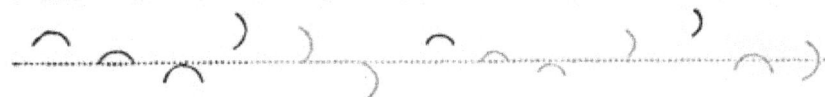

2. ĕmr, ămr, ămr, ŏmr, ŏmr, oomr, ĭmr, ĕmr, ămr, ŭmr, ĭmr, oimr, oumr.

Change the order in which the final consonants *mr* occur, and repeat, thus:

ĕrm, ărm, ărm, ŏrm, ŏrm, oorm, ĭrm, ĕrm, ărm, ŭrm, ĭrm, oirm, ourm.

By this process of transposing final consonants, the function of each phonic, which still remains the same in form, is increased two, and sometimes three fold.

3. ŏml, ăml, äml, ônıl, ŏml, ooml, ĭml, ĕml, ăml, ŭml, ĭml, oiml, oulm

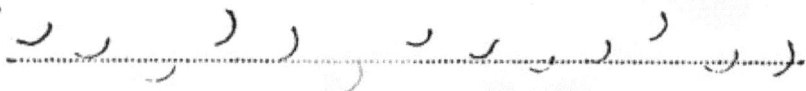

Transpose *ml* to *lm* and repeat, ēlm, ălm, älm, etc.

THIRD GROUP.

The third group is similar to the second except that the curve is reversed, which indicates the addition of the consonant *n* to the vowels and the combinations, thus:

1. ŏne, āne, än, ŏn, ŏwn, oon, ĭn, ĕn, ăn, ŭn, ĭne, oin, oun.

2. ĕnr, änr, änr, ônr, ŏwnr, oonr, ĭnr, ĕnr, ănr, ŭnr, ĭnr, oinr, cunr.

Transpose *nr* to *rn* and repeat, ērn, ūru, ärn, etc.

3. ĕnl, änl, änl, ônl, ŏnl, oonl, ĭnl, ĕnl, änl, ŭnl, ĭnl, oinl, ounl.

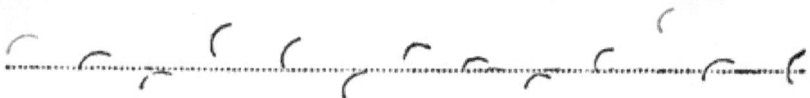

Transpose *nl* to *ln* and repeat, ēln, äln, äln, etc.

PRACTICAL EXERCISE.

aim, emm, am, ene, on, own, in, an, honor, owner, inner,

arm, alum, earn, iron.

SECTION III.

TRANSPOSITION OF THE VOWEL.—The curves in the second and the third group are nearly semi-circles, which indicates that the vowel comes first in the combination. When the curve is flattened to a semi-ellipse, it indicates that the vowel comes last in the combination.

SECOND GROUP.

1   mŏ, mā, mä, mò mō, moo, mĭh, mĕh, mäh, mŭh, mī, moi, mou.

2. mĕre, māre, mär, mór, mòre, moor, mĭr, mĕr, mär, mŭr, mīre, moir, mour.

3. mĕle, māle, mäl, mól, mòle, mool, mĭl, mĕl, mäl, mŭl, mīle, moil, moul.

THIRD GROUP.

1. nĕ, nāy, nä, naw, nò, noo, nĭh, nĕh, näh, nŭh, nīgh, noi, nou.

2. nĕre, nāre, när, nór, nòre, noor, nĭr, nĕr, när, nŭr, nīre, noir, nour.

3. nĕle, nāle, näl, nòl, nòle, nool, nĭl, nĕl, näl, nŭl, nīle, noil, noul.

PRACTICAL EXERCISE.

me, may, maw, mow, moo, my, mow, mere, mare, mar, more, moor.

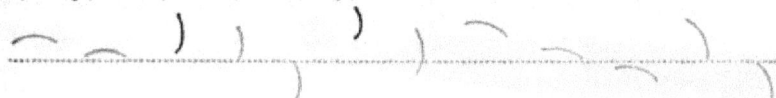

myrrh, mire, meal, male, maul, mole, mill, mull, mile knee, nay,

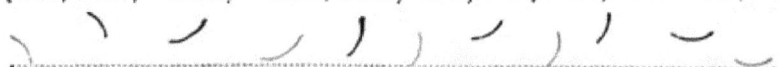

gnaw, no, new, nigh, now, near, nor, nail, knoll, null, nile.

SECTION IV.

ASPIRATED WORDS.—The aspirate *h* is indicated. by a small dot written before the phonic to be aspirated, thus:

he, hay, haw, ho, who, high, how, here, hair, her, hire,

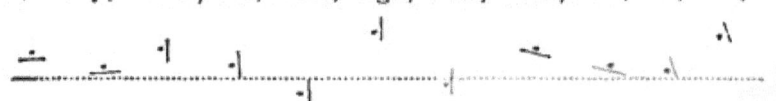

heal, hale, whole, hill, hull, howl, ham, home, whom, him,

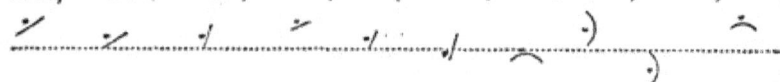

hem, hum, hen, hammer, hemmer, Homer, harm, horn.

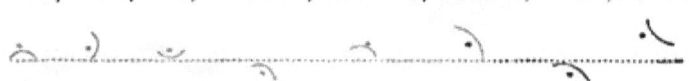

Words of very common occurrence, as he, him, how, etc., are seldom aspirated.

COMPOUND WORDS.—A compound phonic is one composed of two or more simple phonics joined together.

hero, mean, man, miner, alarm, armor, normal.

SENTENCES.

The period is represented by a light oblique line written downward through the line.

The sign of interrogation is represented by a period with a hook turned on the end of it.

The first syllable of a word is frequently written in its proper position, and the second syllable follows without regard to position.

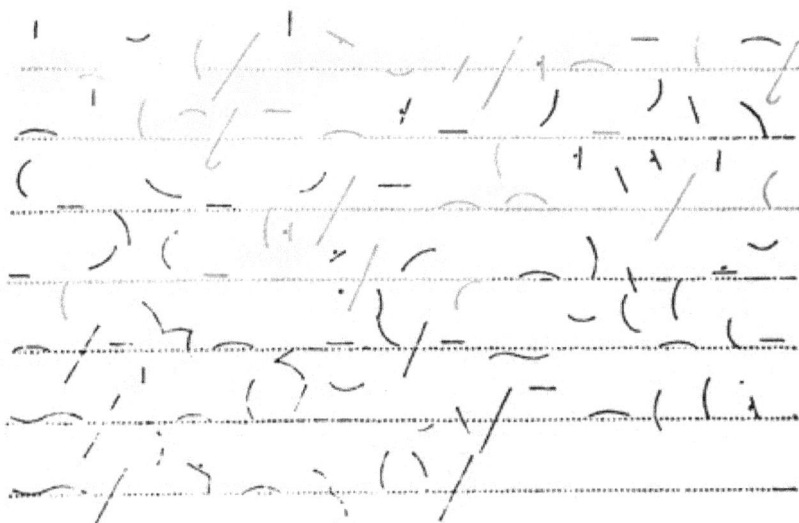

Translation.

I am in now. I hear an owl. How may he know me? May I know him? He may haul a new maul a mile or more on a moor near a new mill. He may aim high or higher. I own a new mill on a high hill. Neal Allen may mow our new hay in May. A Mormon may alarm a miner. A man in honor may earn a name. I may know all in an hour. He may now know her name. My hero may murmur no more.

CHAPTER II.

SECTION II.—T or D.

T or **D** prefixed.—The consonants *t* and *d* being nearly alike in sound are represented by the same character, and are prefixed by shading the phonic at the beginning.

FIRST GROUP.

1. dĕ,   dă,   dä,   dŏ,   dóe,   doo,   dī,   dĕ,   dă,   dŭ,   dīe,   doi,   dou.

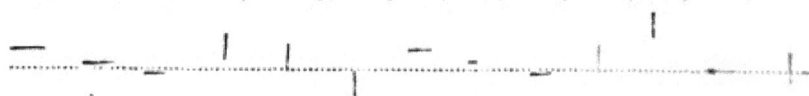

2. tĕre, tăre, tär, tŏr, tŏre, toor, tīr, tĕr, tär, tŭr, tīre, toir, tour.

Transpose *e* and *r* and repeat, trĕ, trā, trä, etc.

3. dĕle, dăle, däl, dôl, dŏle, dool, dīl, dĕl, däl, dŭl, dīle, doil, doul.

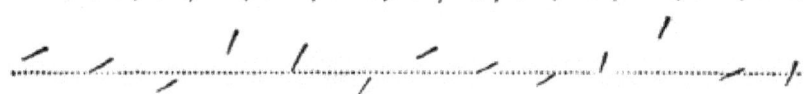

SECOND GROUP.

1. tĕme, tăme, täm, tŏm, tŏme, toom, tīm, tĕm, täm, tŭm, tīme, toim, toum.

2. dĕmr, dämr, dämr, dŏmr, dŏmr, doomr, dīmr, dĕmr, dämr, **dŭmr**, dīmr, [doimr, doumr.

Transpose *e* and *r* and repeat, drĕm, dräm, dräm, drŏm, drŏm, droom.

3. dēml, dāml, däml, dȯnl, dònl, doonl, dĭml, dĕml, dăml, dŭml, dĭml,
doinl, dounl.

THIRD GROUP.

1. dēne, dāne, däu, dȯn, dòne, doon, dĭn, dĕn, dăn, dŭn, dīne, doin, doun.

2. tēnr, tānr, tänr, tònr, tōnr, toonr, tĭnr, tĕnr, tänr, tŭnr, tīnr, toïnr, tounr.

Transpose *nr* to *rn* and repeat, tērn, tārn, tärn, etc.
Transpose *r* and *e* and repeat, trēn, trän, trän, etc.

3. dēnl, dänl, dänl, dònl, dònl, doonl, dīnl, dĕnl, dänl, dŭnl, dīnl, doinl, dounl.

Transpose *nl* to *ln* and repeat, dēln, däln, däln, etc.

PRACTICAL EXERCISE.

tea, day, dough, die, dear, dare, door, dower, deal,

tale, tall, tool, toil, towel, deem, dame, dome, doom, dim,

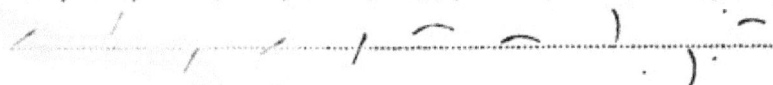

time, dream, dram, drum, dean, ten, dine, drain, drown.

SECTION II.

T OR **D** ADDED.—*T* or *d* is added by shading a phonic at the end.

FIRST GROUP.

1. ēte, āte, ät, ot, ōte, oot, it, et, at, ut, ite, oit, out.

ēdr, ădr, ädr, ôdr, ōdr, oodr, ĭdr, ĕdr, ădr. ûdr, ĭdr, oidr, oudr.

Transpose *dr* to *rd* and repeat, ērd, ārd, ärd, etc.

3. ētl, ātl, ätl, ôtl, ōtl, ootl, ĭtl, ĕtl, ätl, ûtl, ĭtl, oitl, outl.

Transpose *tl* to *lt* and repeat, ēlt, ält, ält, etc.

SECOND GROUP.

1. ēmd, āmd, ämd, ômd, ōmd, oomd, ĭmd, ĕmd, ämd, ûmd, ĭmd, oimd, oumd.

2. ēmrt, āmrt, ämrt, ômrt, ōmrt, oomrt, ĭmrt, ĕmrt, ämrt, ûmrt, ĭmrt, [oimrt, oumrt.

Transpose the last two final consonants *mr* to *rm* and repeat, ērmt, ārmt, ärmt, etc.

Transpose the last two final consonants *rt* to *tr* and repeat, ēmtr, āmtr, ämtr, etc.

3. ōmld, ŭmld, ämld, ômld, ōmld, oomld, ĭmld, ĕmld, ămld, ŭmld, ĭmld.
Loimld, oumld.

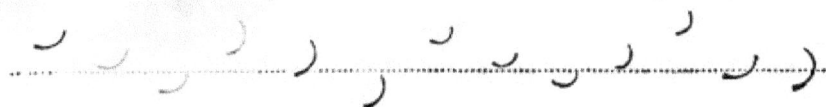

Transpose *ml* to *lm* and repeat, ĕlmd, ălmd, älmd, etc.
Transpose *ld* to *dl* and repeat, ēmdl, āmdl, ämdl, etc.

Third Group.

1. ēnd, ănd, änd, ônd, ōnd, oond, ĭnd, ĕnd, ănd, ŭnd, ĭnd, oind, ound.

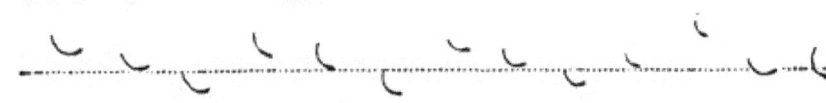

2. ēnrt, ānrt, änrt, ônrt, ōnrt, oonrt, ĭnrt, ĕnrt, ănrt, ŭnrt, ĭnrt, oinrt, ounrt.

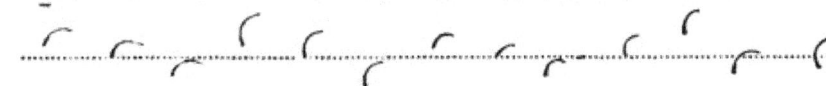

Transpose *nr* to *rn* and repeat, ērnt, ārnt, ärnt, etc.
Transpose *rt* to *tr* and repeat, ēntr, āntr, äntr, etc.

3. ēnlt, ănlt, änlt, ônlt, ōnlt, oonlt, ĭnlt, ĕnlt, ănlt, ŭnlt, ĭnlt, oinlt, ounlt.

Transpose *nl* to *ln* and repeat, ēlnt, ālnt, älnt, etc.
Transpose *lt* to *tl* and repeat, ēntl, āntl, äntl, etc.

Transposition of the Vowel.

Second Group.

1. mede, made, mad, mod, mode, mood, mid, med, mad, mud, mide, moid, moud.

2. mĕtr, mātr, mätr, môtr, mōtr, mootr, mĭtr, mētr, mätr, mütr, mītr, moitr, [moutr.

Transpose *tr* to *rt* and repeat, mĕrt, mārt, märt, etc.

3. mĕdl, mādl, mädl, môdl, mōdl, moodl, mĭdl, mēdl, mädl, müdl, mīdl, [moidl, moudl.

Transpose *dl* to *ld* and repeat, mĕld, mäld, müld, etc.

THIRD GROUP.

1. nete, nate, nat, not, note, noot, nit, net, nat, nut, nite, noit, nout.

2. nĕtr, nātr, nätr, nôtr, nōtr, nootr, nĭtr, nētr, nätr, nütr, nītr, noitr, noutr.

Transpose *tr* to *rt* and repeat, nĕrt, närt, närt, etc.

3. nĕdl, nädl, nädl, nôdl, nōdl, noodl, nĭdl, nēdl, nädl, nüdl, nīdl. [noidl, noudl.

Transpose *dl* to *ld* and repeat, nĕld, näld, näld, etc.

PRACTICAL EXERCISE.

cat, ate, at, odd, ode, hid, heat, hide, heater, heard,

art, odor, ailed, old, oiled, howled, held,

end, owned, hunt, hound, honored, earned, hunter, hammered, meed,

made, mad, mode, mood, mite, metre, matter, mutter, mart, mort,

nailed, malt, mold, mild, melt, middle, need, not, note, net,

nut, night, neater, kneeled, nailed, moored.

SECTION III.

T OR D PREFIXED AND ADDED.—Shading a phonic its entire length indicates that it begins with *t* or *d*, and ends with the same.

FIRST GROUP.

1. dede, dade, dad, dod, dode, dood, did, ded, dād, dud, dide, doid, dond.

2. tētr, tātr, tätr, tôtr, tōtr, tootr, ŭtr, tĕtr, tătr, tŭtr, tĭtr, teitr, toatr.

Transpose *e* and *r* and repeat, trēt, trāt, trät, etc.
Transpose *tr* to *rt* and repeat, tērt, tärt, tärt, etc.

3. dēdl, dādl, dädl, dôdl, dōdl, doodl, dĭdl, dĕdl, dădl, dŭdl, dĭdl, doidl, dondl,

Transpose *dl* to *ld* and repeat, dēld, dāld, däld, etc.

Second Group.

1. dēmd, dămd, dämd, dômd, dŏmd, doomd, dĭmd, dĕmd, dămd, dŭmd,
[dīmd, doimd, doumd.

2. dēmrd, dămrd, dämrd, dômrd, dŏmrd, doomrd, dĭmrd, dĕmrd, dămrd, dŭmrd,
[dīmrd, doimrd, doumrd.

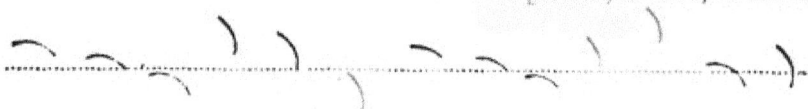

Transpose *e* and *r* and repeat, drēmd, drămd, drämd, etc.

3. dēmlt, dămlt, dämlt, dômlt, dŏmlt, doomlt, dĭmlt, dĕmlt, dămlt, dŭmlt,
[dīmlt, doimlt, doumlt.

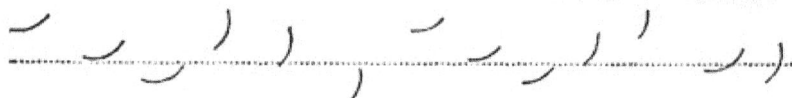

Third Group.

1. tēnd, tănd, tänd, tônd, tŏnd, toond, tĭnd, tĕnd, tănd, tŭnd, tīnd, toind, tound.

2. tēnrd, tănrd, tänrd, tônrd, tŏnrd, toonrd, tĭnrd, tĕnrd, tănrd, tănrd, tīnrd,
[toinrd, tounrd.

Transpose *nr* to *rn* and repeat, tērnd, tărnd, tärnd, etc.

Transpose *e* and *r* and repeat, trēnd, trănd, tränd, etc.

- 3. tēnld, tănld, tänld, tônld, tŏnld, toonld, tĭnld, tĕnld, tănld, tănld, tīnld,
[toinld, tounld

PRACTICAL EXERCISE.

deed, date, dote, died, **tart, tort, towered,** treat, **trait,**

trot, dirt, dolt, toiled, deemed, **tamed,** doomed, **timed,**

dreamed, drummed, trimmed, drained, tend, tanned, drowned, turned.

Words selected from advanced lessons for present use.

the, from, of, **his, is,** has, as, for, **was, with,** and.

SENTENCES.

NOTE.—The past tense of verbs is often omitted when the context will supply it.

Translation.

The heat from the hot iron made the model melt. He heard of the murder at midnight. I held my hat in my hand. His name is Howard. Maud, our new maid, has no needle. At the hour of ten in the night he was a mile or more from home. He ought to mould the metal in the night. The end of the metal handle was ironed. I heard the mild murmur of the mermaid. I owed the moulder a mite for metal. The mat was aired and the odor of the oil was milder. Tom met the dame at the turn of the hill. He told me to tell the old tale.

CHAPTER III.

SECTION I.

The **W** Hook.—The initial and final consonant *w* is represented by a small hook joined to the under side of horizontal and to the left of vertical phonics. The *w* hook, when joined to curves, is an initial only—never final.

1. weed, wade, wood, wed, wait, wit, weaned, waned, wound.

2. wine, wend, won, wind, ware, war, wore, wire, water.

3. warm, warn, worn, wierd, wired, wart, warmed, warrant, winter.

4. wield, wail, wall, will, well, wool, wild, wailed, weal.

Final **N.**—By doubling the length of a curve the consonant *n* is added; thus, mean, **men,** man, meant, **moan, non, none,** noun, noon.

THE INDEFINITE VOWEL.—**Many words begin** or end with a **vowel having the sound of** ĭ or ŭ. **This** indefinite vowel is represented by a short light tick written in either a horizontal or a vertical direction ; thus :

6. muddy, **eighty, weary, annoy, weighty, mighty, award, witty, haughty.**

This indefinite vowel is **frequently omitted by the reporter when it** would not **involve a sacrifice of legibility.**

SECTION II.

The **R** Hook.—The **initial and final consonant** *r* **is** represented by a **large hook similar to the** *w* **hook, but doubled in** size.

ray, raw, row, rye, reed, raid, road, rood, rid.

round, rain, renewed, remote, remain, retain, retainer, return, ream.

runner, reamer, roomer, **render, remit,** reared, rare, roar.

roll, real, rail, rule, royal, rolled, error, **mirror.**

horror, **holder,** moulder, **milder, herder,** railer, reamed, remote.

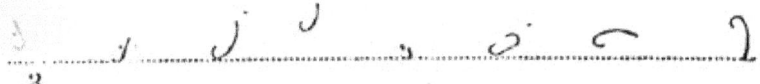

3

Final **ING.**—The final syllable *ing* is represented by a small dot at the end of the phonic ; thus,

hearing, hailing, willing, waiting, dealing, nearing, netting.

The plural of *ing* is represented by a small circle at the end of a phonic ; thus,

winnings, earnings, windings, wanderings, mouldings, dealings.

Selected Words.

there, have, after, came, come, a or an, by, could, you.

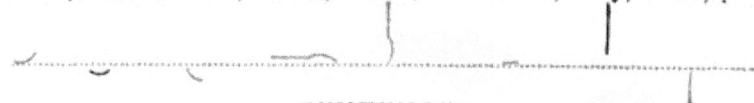

Sentences.

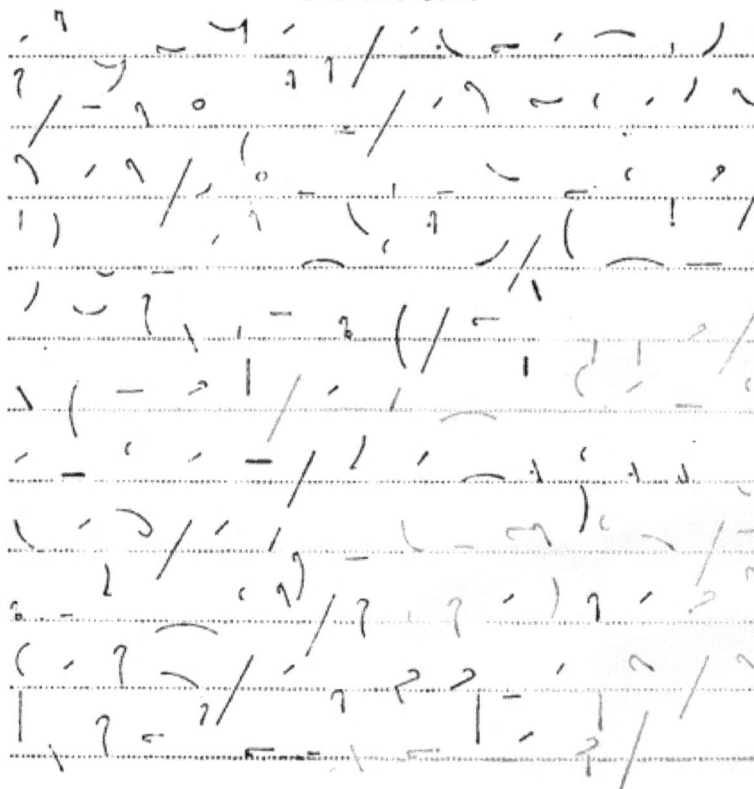

Translation.

The *wild animal went into the wood. The hunter weighed the meat, and mulled the wine. He wore his new white hat The warm wind of the mild winter warmed the water. There is a newer and a neater way of doing this. I might have had the wire made of white metal. Nine men †came a mile in one hour, and it was noon We tried to do well. Toward noon he will come. The old man died on the day of the date of the deed. Molly, the maid, heard of her error after turning the mirror. The old woman had earned a reward of merit. He was a mighty man of war. Round and round the dome rode the reeling rider on the roan mare. The rude railer railed at the good reader. Wearied by our run, we whiled away an hour waiting by the railroad.

CHAPTER IV.

SECTION I.

CHAY and **JAY.**—The consonants *chay,* and *jay,* initial and final, being nearly alike in sound, are represented by a small hook similar to the *w* hook, but joined to the upper side of horizontal, and to right side of vertical phonics. When the *chay* and *jay* hook is joined to curves as a final it is turned to the inner side of the curve.

NOTE.—The past tense of verbs is often omitted when the context will supply it.

gee,   jay,   jaw,   chew,   joy,   Jim,   gem,   jam,   chain.

John,   June,   gin,   join,   each,   hatch,   watch,   midge,   match.

---

* The phonic has the *r* inclination ; it should have the *l* inclination.
† *Came* and *come* are frequently abbreviated in reporting, by omitting the last part of the phonic.

much,   rich, which, niche, cheer, chair, chore, charm, churn.

teacher, touch, jail, jailed, child, challenge, knowledge, millage.

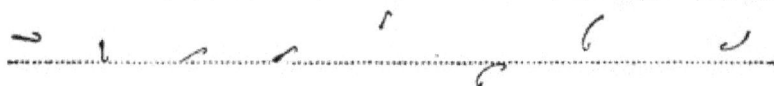

SECTION II.

The CONSONANT L.—The consonant *l* is represented by
by a large hook, joined to the same side of the phonic as the
chay and *jay,* but double the size of *chay* and *jay.*

leech,   latch,   lead,   lay,   law,   low,   lid,   lad,   lie.

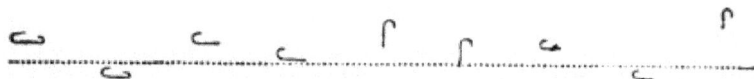

lame,   loam,   loom,   leaned, lane, loin, loaned, line, leer.

lower,   liar, laurel, lurch, large, world, earl, churl, herald.

lilly,   lull,   little,   lonely, landlord, lantern, tenderly.

journal, go, get, be,   can, got, but,   put.

SENTENCES.

Translation.

Knowledge is a jewel. Richard, the rich man, ran away from home. After ten in the night the wind changed. The danger the intelligent gentleman was in was imaginary. He was charged not to judge the man by his manner. Her gent'e manner cheated the unwary woman Go tell him the dream we dreamed The man had no doubt as to his duty in the matter. The little lad wandered near the water. The world is not all harmony. He wrote a witty letter to the lady. The learned rhymer leaned his arm on the railing which lay in the running water. The light haired man wanted a larger load of lead. We heard the low moaning of the wind on the mountain. **I intend to try** my hand at tearing down **the** old wall. **The trader did trade** away his trained trotter. He managed the matter right well.

CHAPTER V.

THE **F** AND **V** CURVE.

Th consonants *f* and *v*, both initial and final, are represented by a small light curve, similar to the *m* and the *n* curve, but distinguished from them by **being much shorter.**

If the curve is made nearly a semi-circle it indicates that the vowel comes first, if it is flattened, the vowel comes last.

fee, feed, fade, fought, vote, foot, fight, fame, foam, vim.

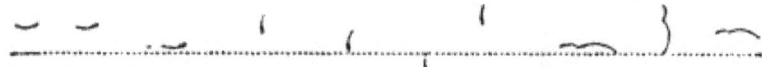

famed, feigned, fine, found, move, muff, knave, knife, miff.

fear, fair, far, for, four, fire, fort, feared, ford, dove, void.

fairly, fairer, farmer, *forge, *verge, foreign, feel, fail, fall.

fallen, never, novel, naval, forward, wharfage, roof, ravel.

rover, lover, final, flame, frame, fruit, freight, fright, fled.

* **Supply** the *jay* hook to the phonics.

flood, floor, flare.

It will be observed from the examples above that the f and v curve is written like either the m or the n curve.

The particular form to be used in representing words is a matter of convenience entirely, and the student will learn from experience, as he advances, which form is most convenient.

SENTENCES.

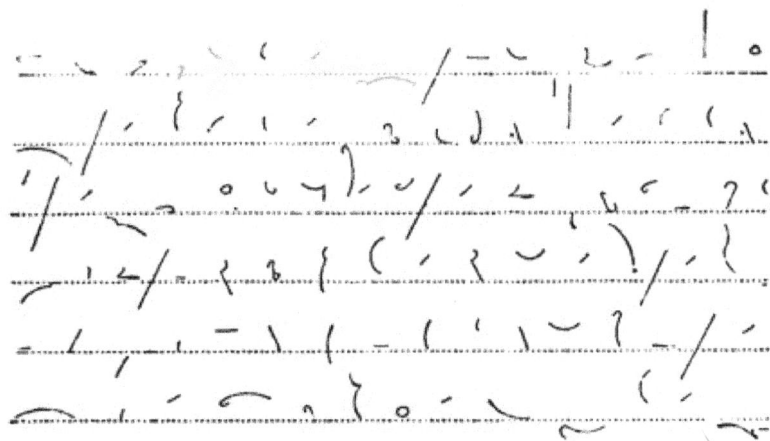

Translation.

We fared well without fear of the famine. He feared to offend him by his manner. The fond feeling of the woman was very much hurt by the fall of her idol. The farmer fetched his forage into the village. The fleet footed churl filched a roll of flannel and fled. A flower was found on the floor in the morning. The miner had a dull tool, and he tore down a ton of dirt in one day. The men and the women were frightened as the train ran on the tram-way.

CHAPTER VI.

INITIAL AND FINAL S, ST, STR, SL AND SP.

Initial and final **S** is represented by a small circle joined to the upper side of horizontal, and to the right side of vertical phonics of the first group, and to the inside of the curves of the second and the third group.

see,   say,   saw, sow, sight,   sat,   seed,   sod,   seem,   same.

some,   sane,   sun, sign, sinned, send, sand, house,   eyes,   ace.

mace, mice, mouse, nice,   seer,   soar,   sire,   sour,   summer.

simmer, smear,   snear,   snore,   horse,   source, force, remorse,   worse.

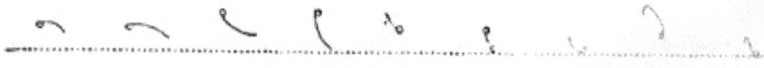

seal,   sail,   soul,   soil,   solemn,   small,   smell,   snail, smile.

ST is represented by a circle double the size of the *s* circle.

stay, stow, stew, steam, stem, stamen, stain, stone, stunned.

east, host, most, missed, massed, ceased, leased, last, roast.

roused, hoist, restore, steamer, stormy, sternly, fast, faster.

store, stair, stear, steal, stole, stool, stale, stall, style.

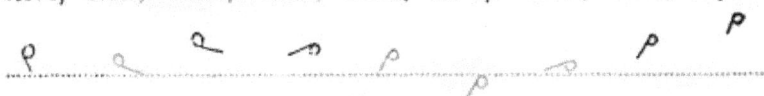

STR is represented by a circle double the size of the *st* circle.

stray, straw, stream, strain, easter, oyster, mister, muster, muster.

SL is represented by a small semi-circle turned either to the right or the left.

slay, slow, sly, slim, slam, slain, sledge, slayer, slur.

SP is represented by a small, flat initial loop joined to the upper side of horizontal, and the right side of vertical phonics of the first group, and to the inside of curves. It is never used as a final.

speed, spade, spot, spat, spite, spear, spare, spire, spoil.

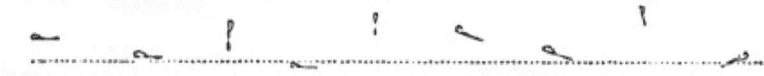

splutter, spill, spin, spun, span, spine, Spain, sprain, spurn.

SENTENCES.

Translation.

Our horse being lame, we remained over night at a wayside inn. In autumn many leaves turn red. The seal of the signer was in the centre. The silent suffering of the wounded softened the hearts of even their enemies. The very winds and waves listened to his voice. The winds have voices and the waves have faces. They ascended the distant mountain, and read the doom of their race in the setting sun. We saw a sly smile on his slim slender face. The slim lad with the sled slid down the icy hill. In the splutter,* the handsome lady from Spain spoiled the splendid scenery. There are many men of one mind.

---

*Supply the *r* hook to the phonic.

CHAPTER VII.

INITIAL AND FINAL TH, THR AND YEH.

TH is represented by a short, light tick, written obliquely downward to the left, or obliquely upward to the right.

thee, they, thaw, though, **thy**, **thou**, **theme**, **them**, **thumb**.

then, than, thine, thin, thorn, theorem, therein, **there**, **thirst**.

theory, theatre, thirdly, thill, thinly, north, **south**, thought, seethe.

THR is represented by a short, light curve, written obliquely upward to the right. Both forms of the curve are used. The word *with* is simply the *th* tick with the *w* hook prefixed. The same phonic, written through the line and shaded, represents *without*. *That* is simply the *th* tick written under the line and shaded.

three, **through**, **throughout**, thread, **thrust**, **thrall**, **with**, that, without

YEH is represented by a short, light curve, about half the length of the *thr* curve, written obliquely upward to the right.

ye, yea, you, year, **yore**, yacht, **yellow**, yield, **yonder**.

SENTENCES.

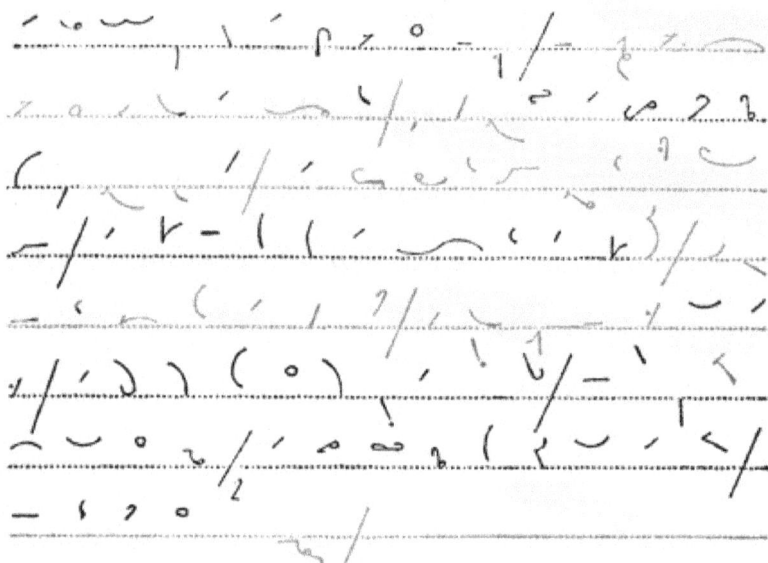

Translation.

The fierce Indian who uttered the loud yell is a Ute. A
thousand yellow men yelled as they entered the enemy's fort.
That old yarn which the sailor related was only a yarn after
all. The lady sent for three yards of white linen thread.
The author did not know the name of the other volume.
There are eight of them on the old wall. They entered
through a hole in the hull. The drummer drummed on his
drum during the trying ordeal. He tried to thwart him in
his efforts. The silly speech was not delivered in the theatre.
He fought with his wily adversary.

CHAPTER VIII.

INITIAL AND FINAL SW, SH, SHN, SESSION
AND NG.

SW is represented by a small circle joined to the under side
of horizontal, and to the left side of vertical phonics of the

first group, and to the back or convex side of curves of the
second and the third group.

sway, sweet, sweat, swaddle, swim, swam, swain, swale, swell.

swarm, swimmer, swan swindle, sworn, swine, swift, swerve.

SH is represented by beginning or ending the *s* or the *sw*
circle with a small back hook running through the line.

she, show, shaw, shy, shame, sham, shone, shear, share.

shine, shimmer, shiner, shore, sure, shell, shall, shadow, surely.

SHN is used as a final syllable only, and is similar to *sh*
but the hook is doubled in size.

vision, fashion, motion, notion, ocean, ration, hash, national, sash.

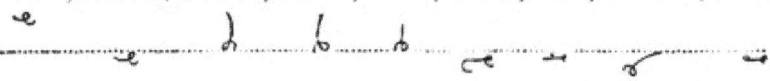

emotional, missioner, measurement, nourishment.

SESSION or **SITION** is represented by a large loop joined
to either side of straight phonics, and to the inside of curves.

physician, musician, transition, cessation, decision.

NG or **NK** is represented by a long straight mark, about
half an inch in length, and written in the same directions as
the phonics of the first group.

ink, sing, ring, rung, long, song, swing, longer.

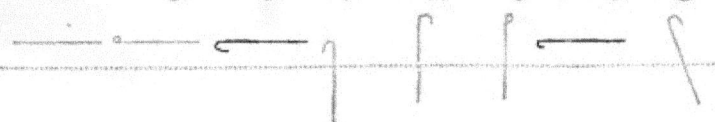

4

449454

SENTENCES.

Translation.

The good swimmer swam a mile on the swell of the waves.
The swollen waters swung the vessel in towards the shore.
The sweet singer sang a sweet song while swinging in the
swing. After being lawfully sworn, the witness swore that he
did not see the lady swoon. The shy man shunned the
shining sun on the shore while fishing for shad. They have
our good wishes without* malice. The shrewd fellow uttered a
shrill whistle. It was not the sentry's intention to shoot
the officer; the shooting was not intentional. A dram was
drained from the tank down by the dam. A drunk man

*The phonic has the *jay* hook; it should have the *w* hook.

dreamed that he drew a drowning man out of the water.
Error must yield, however strongly it may be defended. The
learned physician and the musician, while in a state of transition, fortified their decision by a cessation of hostilities.

CHAPTER IX.

SECTION I.

The Consonants P, B, K and GAY.

The consonants *p* and *b* are represented by a straight
stroke about three-eighths of an inch in length.

B may be distinguished from *p* by drawing a short
oblique line across the phonic.

When a word is represented by a compound phonic, the
first part of the phonic is written in its proper position, and
the second part follows without regard to position.

bee, pay, paw, bow, peer, bear, bar, pour, peal.

ball, bowl, pale, peep, pop, pope, bay, papal, bough.

K and **GAY** are represented by a short straight stroke,
about three-sixteenths of an inch in length.

GAY may be distinguished from *k* by a short oblique line
drawn across the phonic.

kee, gay, go, cow, care, grew, greed, great, glade, close.

keep, cape, cap, cop, cope, coop, keeper, cake, clock.

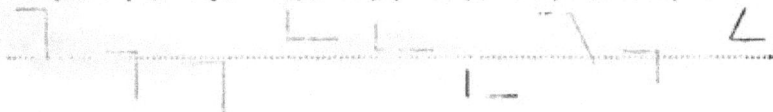

SECTION II.

KW.—The sound represented by *q* in the English orthography is equivalent to *kw*, and is represented by the phonic *k* with the *w* hook attached.

PRACTICAL EXERCISE.

beak, bake, back, bock, poke, hook, baker, poker, cable.

maple, noble, nibble, rebel, rabble, rubber, ballast, bailment.

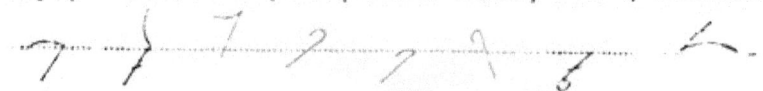

paid, deep, debate, banner, barge, boat, bathe, batter, better.

bayonet, pride, proud, plod, play, parasol, present, depart

kick, kitchen, kiss, keystone, keel, kennel, cat, courage.

goad, case, casement, carriage, cartoon, casket, agony, coal.

ignoble, coal-men, coal-mine, gold-mine, copper, gobble.

costs, coast, cautious, caution, sheep, sheepish, shape, ship.

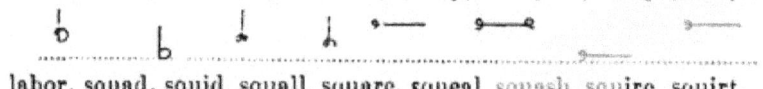

labor, squad, squid, squall, square, squeal, squash, squire, squirt.

SENTENCES.

Translation.

Busied with public affairs, the council would sit for hours smoking and watching the smoke curl from their pipes to the ceiling. In that calm syrian afternoon, memory, a pensive

Ruth, went gleaning the silent fields of childhood, and found the scattered grain still golden, and the morning sunlight *fresh and fair. Dying for a principle is a higher degree of virtue than scolding for it. If ever you saw a crow with a king-bird after him, you have an image of a dull speaker and a lively listener. It is true that the glorious sun pours down his golden flood as cheerily on the poor man's cottage as on the rich man's palace. When a man becomes overheated by working, running, rowing or making furious speeches, the six or seven millions of perspiration tubes pour out their fluid and the whole body is bathed and cooled. The men whom men respect, the women whom women approve, are the men and women who bless their species. Sweet was the sound, when oft, at evening's close, up yonder hill the village murmur rose; there, as I passed with careless steps and slow, the mingling notes came softened from below.

---

*Complete *sh* by supplying the *sh* hook.

CHAPTER X.

EXPEDIENTS.

The vowel I and the diphthong OI, as well as phonics in which these sounds occur, may be written upward occasionally when it is desired to give a more distinct vocalization to a word.

Ohio, admire, rely, realize, July, toy, boy, coy, destroy.

When it is desired to indicate clearly the position of the vowel in a word, it may be done by separating the vowel from the consonant by drawing a short line through the phonic.

ape, ache, rock, leak, hope, seek, eager, equal, pay.

PREFIXES.

COM and **CON** are indicated by a short shaded mark, written obliquely downward to the right or the left.

comply, complain, comprehend, contain, condone, confuse, confound.

The prefix **CONTRA** is represented by a short heavy mark, written in a horizontal or a vertical direction.

contradict, **contract, contributory**, contravene, controversy.

EX is represented by a small tick written obliquely downward to the right, or upward to the left.

exert, exalt, **extort,** express, exhaust, **exist**, exchange.

The indefinite vowel is used to represent *a, an* or *and,* and the *th* tick to represent *they* or *the,* at the beginning or the end of a word. When the *sur* circle is used as a final it becomes *urs* and represents *was.*

may the, a man, the man, they were. ask a, ask the.

hearing a, hearing the, wearing a, wearing the, he was.

there was, there is, that is, that was, was that.

The word *which* is often indicated by the *chay* hook at the beginning or end of a word. *Should* is often indicated by shading the *sh* hook.

of which, for which, which I, which he. which it, which had.

with which, which would, would we, we will, we were, are we.

were we, what we, will have, I shall be, I wish.

I should, I will, who will, should not.

Two words written closely together indicates that the words *of* or *to* is to be understood as coming between them. Several words are frequently joined together in a phrase without lifting the pen from the paper.

The vowel *oo,* or any phonic containing that vowel, when commenced on the line, takes the sound of *u.*

The dash is indicated by a short, horizontal, wavy line.

Applause is indicated by a short, vertical, wavy line.

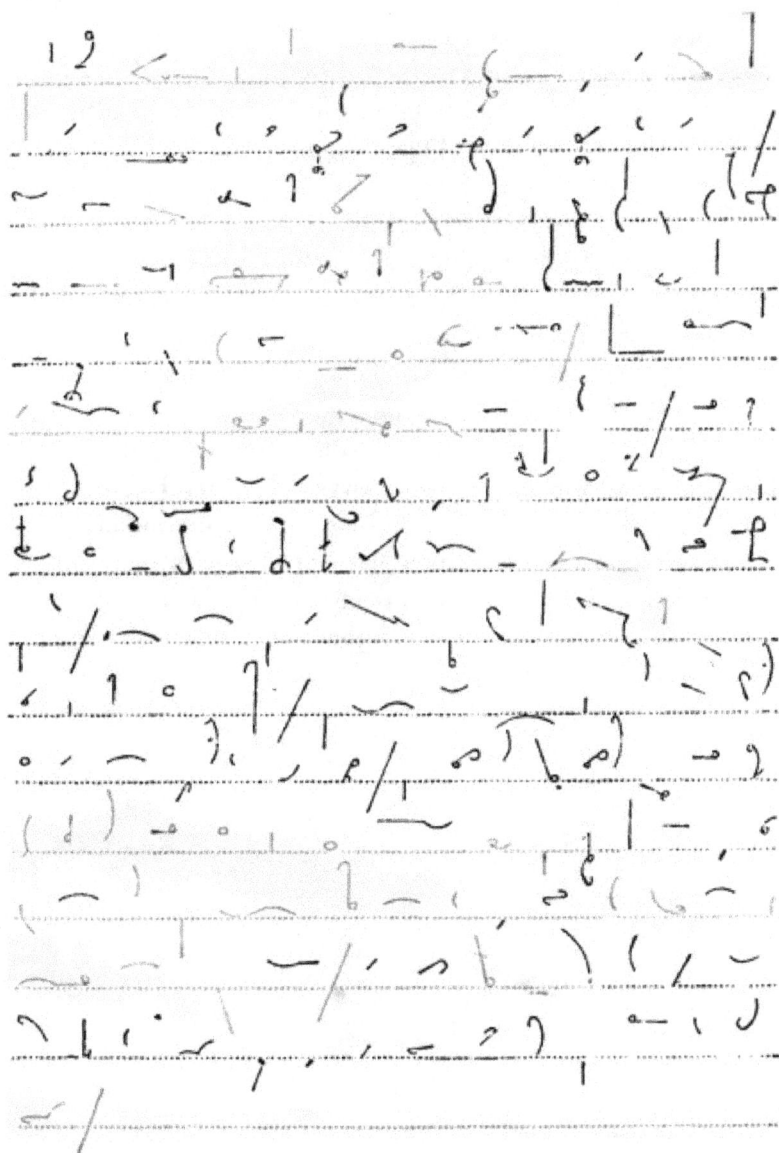

PRACTICAL EXERCISE.

SENTENCES.

Translation.

I solemnly declare — and I do not speak unadvisedly — that the measures adopted by the passage of this resolution will hasten the dissolution of the union. When we carefully consider what appeals to our minds, and exercise upon it our own reason — taking into respectful consideration what others say upon it — and then come to a conclusion of our own, we act as intelligent beings. Pope skimmed the cream of good sense and expression wherever he could find it. It is one of the most marvelous facts in the natural world, that, though hydrogen is highly inflammable, and oxygen is a supporter of combustion, both combined form an element, water, which is destructive to fire. Commend me to the preacher who has learned by experience what are human ills and what is human wrong. Good name in man and woman, my dear Lord, is the immediate jewel of their souls. Who steals my purse steals trash ; 'tis something, nothing ; 'twas mine, 'tis his, and has been slave to thousands ; but he that filches from me my good name, robs me of that which not enriches him, and makes me poor indeed. The little birds at morning dawn, clothed in warm coats of feather, conclude that they away will roam to seek for milder weather.

CHAPTER XI.

DEATH OF LITTLE NELL.

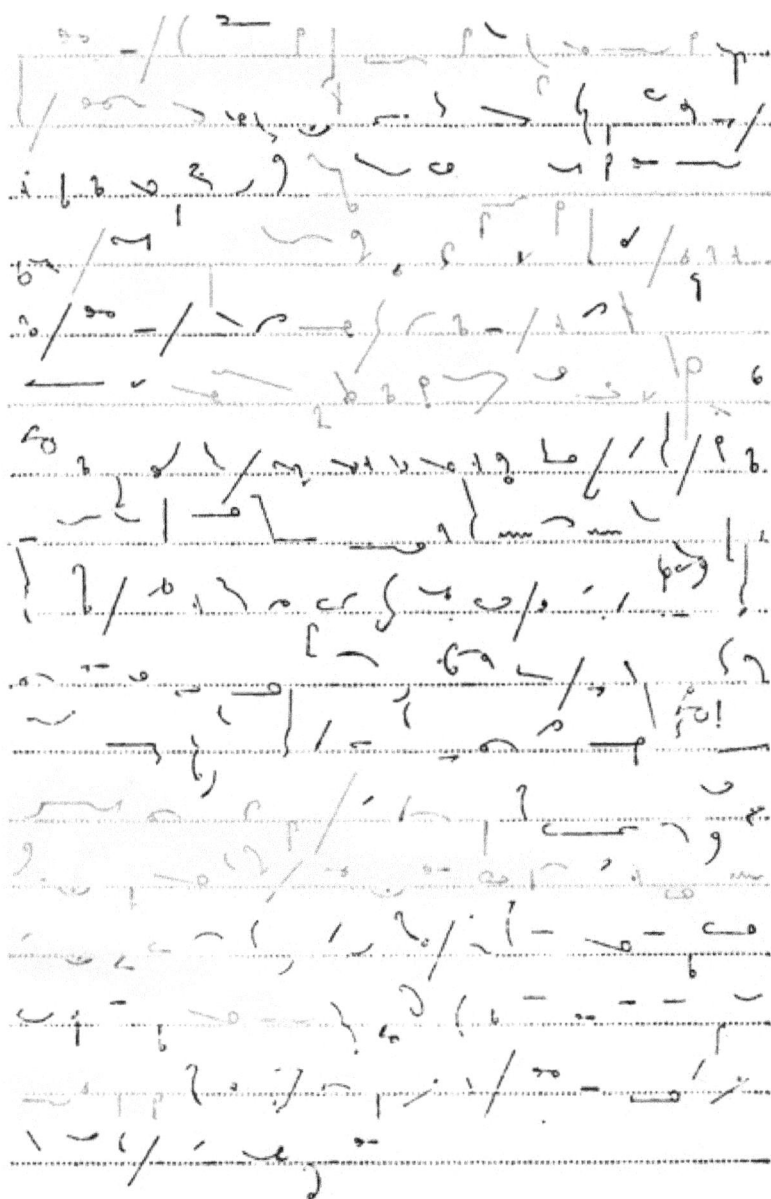

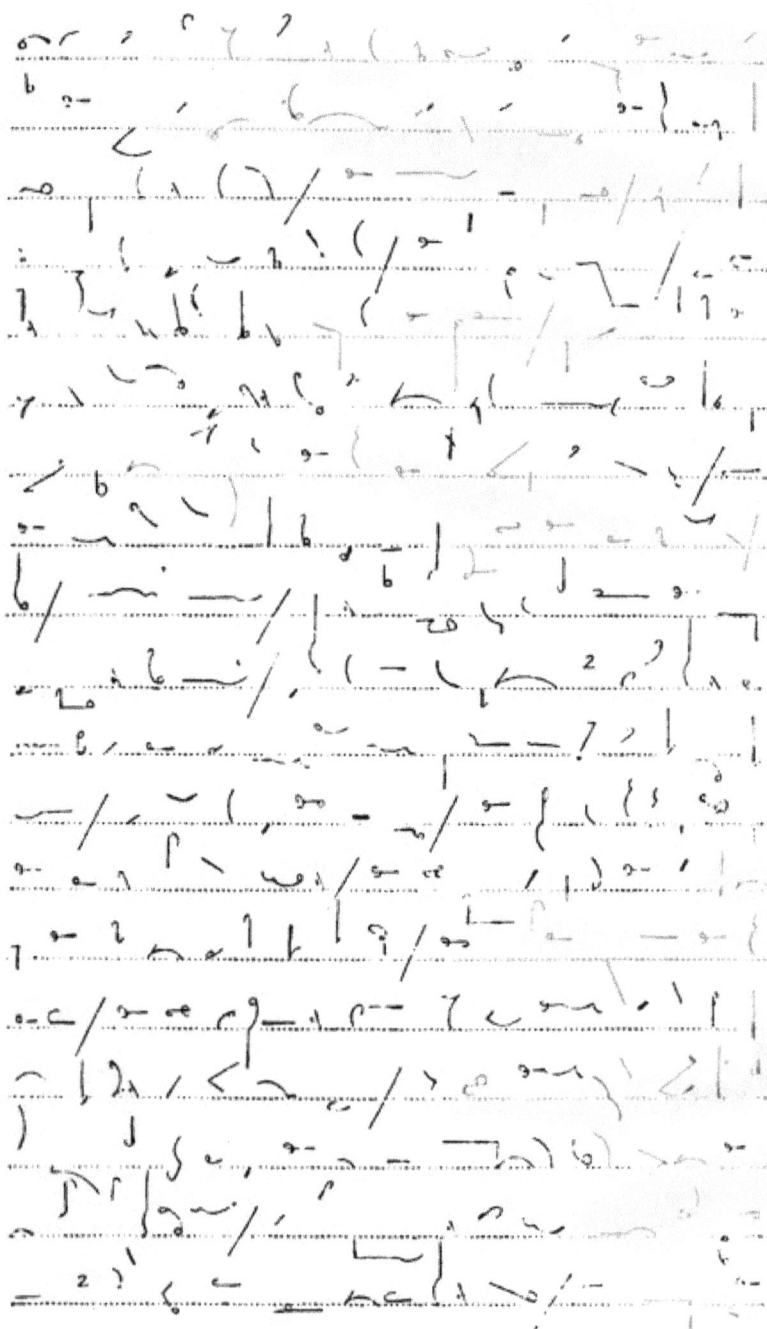

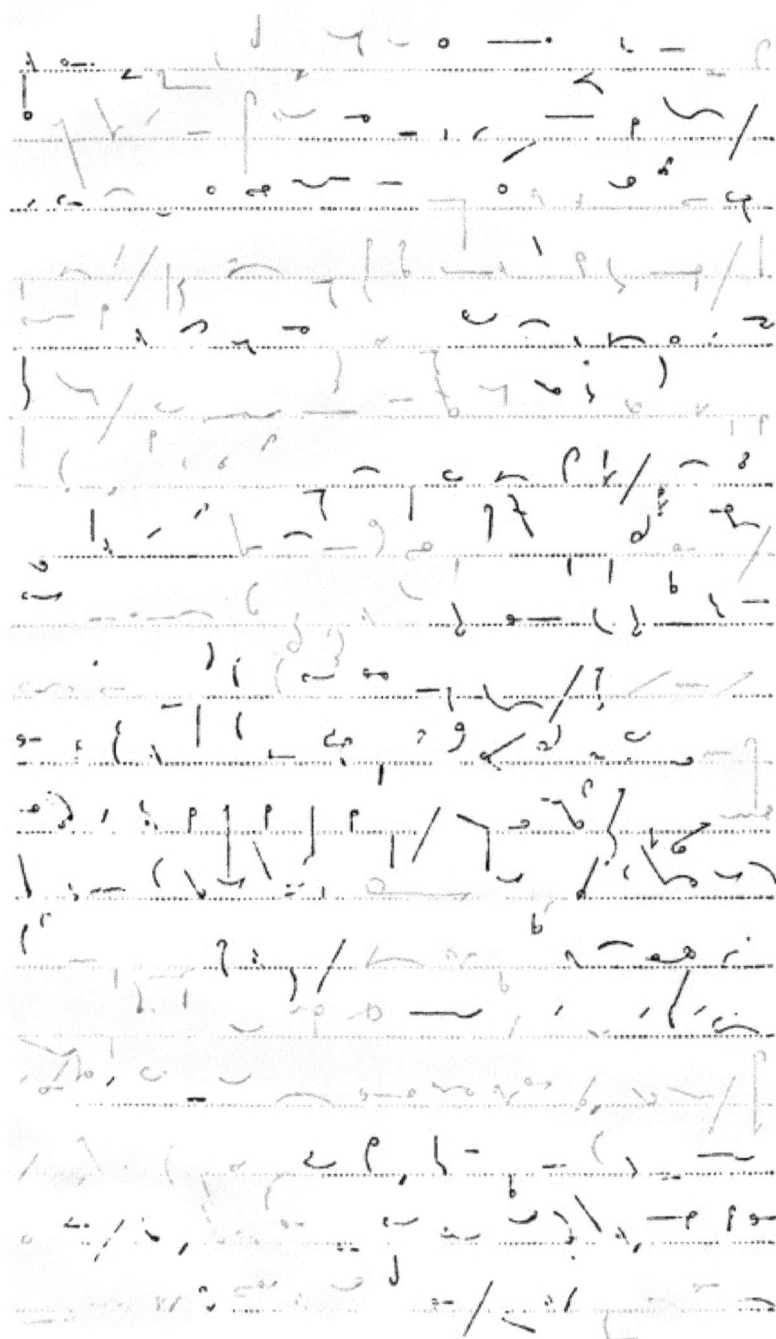

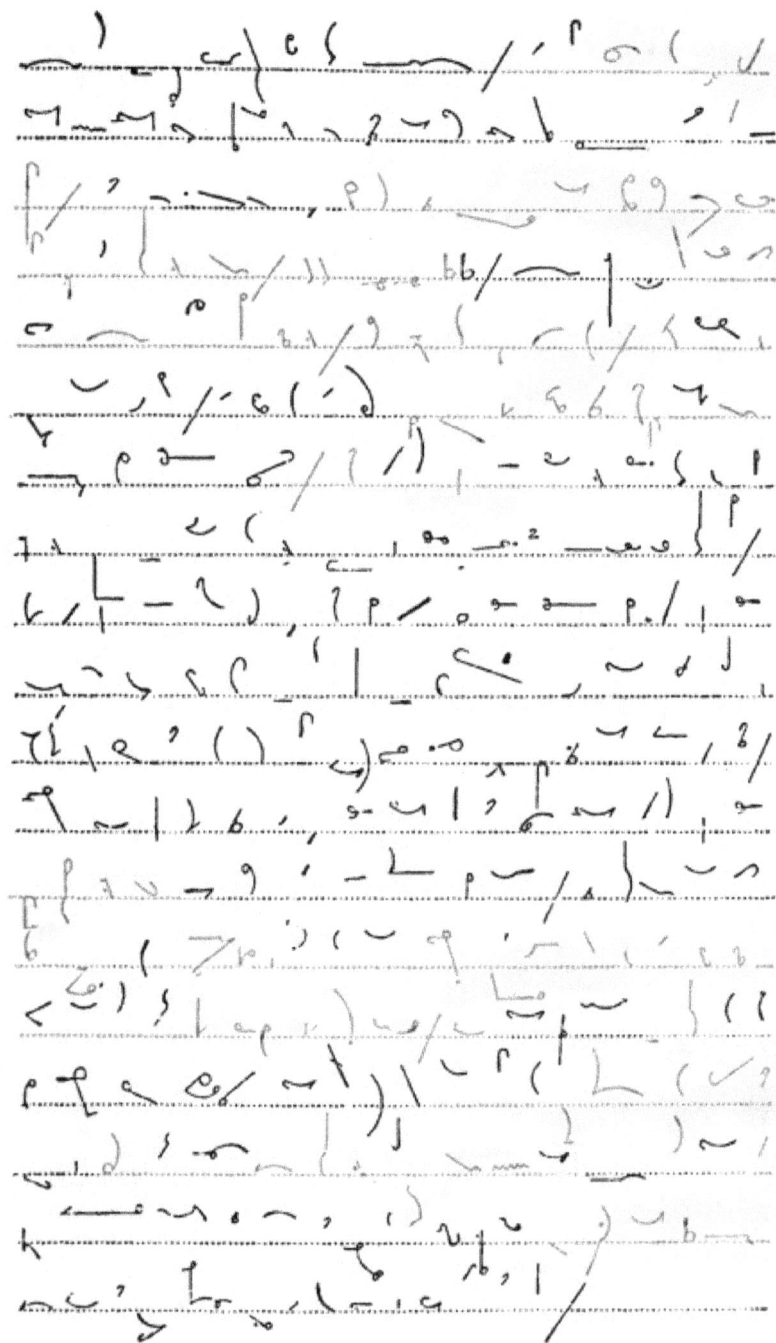

DEATH OF LITTLE NELL.

NOTE.—The following exercise should be copied over and over until the entire exercise can be written from dictation at a speed of, at least, one hundred words per minute.

She was dead. No sleep so beautiful and calm, so free from trace of pain, so fair to look upon. She seemed a creature fresh from the hand of God, and waiting for the breath of life; not one who had lived and suffered death. Her couch was dressed with here and there some winter-berries and green leaves, gathered in a spot she had been used to favor. "When I die, put near me something that has loved the light, and had the sky above it always." Those were her words.

She was dead. Dear, gentle, patient, noble Nell was dead. Her little bird, a poor, slight thing, which the pressure of a finger would have crushed, was stirring nimbly in its cage; and the strong heart of its child-mistress was mute and motionless forever. Where were the traces of her early cares, her sufferings, and fatigues? All gone. Sorrow was dead, indeed, in her; but peace and perfect happiness were born—imaged—in her tranquil beauty and profound repose. And still her former self lay there unaltered in this change.

Yes; the old fireside had smiled upon that same sweet face, which had passed, like a dream, through haunts of misery and care. At the door of the poor school-master on the summer evening, before the furnace-fire upon the cold wet night, at the same still bedside of the dying boy, there had been the same mild, lovely look.

The old man took one languid arm in his, and held the small hand to his breast for warmth. It was the hand she had stretched out to him with her last smile,—the hand that had led him on through all their wanderings. Ever and anon he pressed it to his lips; then hugged it to his breast again, murmuring that it was warmer now; and, as he said it, he looked in agony to those who stood around, as if imploring them to help her.

She was dead, and past all help or need of it. The ancient rooms she had seemed to fill with life, even while her own was waning fast, the garden she had tended, the eyes she had gladdened, the noiseless haunts of many a thoughtful hour, the paths she had trodden, as it were, but yesterday, could know her no more.

She had been dead two days. They were all about her at the time, knowing that the end was drawing on. She died soon after daybreak. They had read and talked to her in the earlier portion of the night, but, as the hours crept on, she sunk to sleep. They could tell, by what she faintly uttered in her dreams, that they were of her journeyings with the old man; they were of no painful-scenes, but of those who had helped and used them kindly; for she often said, "God bless you!" with great fervor. Waking, she never wandered in her mind but once; and that was at beautiful music which she said was in the air. God knows. It may have been.

Opening her eyes at last from a very quiet sleep, she begged that they would kiss her once again. That done, she turned to the old man, with a lovely smile upon her face, —such, they said, as they had never seen, and never could forget—and clung with both arms about his neck. They did not know that she was dead at first.

She had spoken very often of the two sisters, who, she said, were like dear friends to her. She wished they could be told how much she thought about them, and how she had watched them as they walked together by the river-side. She would like to see poor Kit, she had often said of late. She wished there was somebody to take her love to Kit, and even then she never thought or spoke about him but with something of her old, clear, merry laugh.

For the rest, she had never murmured or complained; but, with a quiet mind, and manner quite unaltered, save that she every day became more earnest and more grateful to them, she faded like the light upon the summer's evening.

The child who had been her little friend came there, almost as soon as it was day, with an offering of dried flowers, which he asked them to lay upon her breast. He begged hard to see her, saying that he would be very quiet, and that they need not fear his being alarmed, for he sat alone by his younger brother all day long when he was dead, and had felt glad to be so near him.

They let him have his wish; and, indeed, he kept his word; and was, in his childish way, a lesson to them all. Up to that time the old man had not spoken once,—except to her —or stirred from the bedside. But, when he saw her little favorite, he was moved as they had not seen him yet, and made as though he would have come nearer.

Then, pointing to the bed, he burst into tears for the first time; and they who stood by, knowing that the sight of this child had done him good, left them alone together. Soothing him with his artless talk of her, the child persuaded him to take some rest, to walk abroad, to do almost as he desired him. And when the day came on which they must remove her in her earthly shape from earthly eyes forever, he led him away, that he might not know when she was taken from him.

And now the bell—the bell she had so often heard by night and day, and listened to it with solemn pleasure, almost as a living voice—rung its remorseless toll for her, so young, so beautiful, so good. Decrepit age, and vigorous life, and blooming youth, and helpless infancy, poured forth — on crutches, in the pride of health and strength, in the full blush of promise, in the mere dawn of life—to gather round her tomb.

Old men were there, whose eyes were dim and senses failing; grandmothers, who might have died ten years ago and still been old; the deaf, the blind, the lame, the palsied, the living dead, in many shapes and forms, were there, to see the

closing of that early grave. Along the crowded path they
bore her now, pure as the newly-fallen snow that covered it,
whose day on earth had been as fleeting.

Under that porch, where she had sat when Heaven in its
mercy brought her to that peaceful spot, she passed again;
and the old church received her in its quiet shade. They
carried her to an old nook, where she had many and many
a time sat musing, and laid their burden softly on the pave-
ment. The light streamed on it through the colored window,
—a window where the bows of trees were ever rustling in
the summer, and where the birds sang sweetly all day long.
With every breath of air that stirred among those branches in
the sunshine, some trembling, changing light would fall upon
her grave.

Earth to earth, ashes to ashes, dust to dust ! Many a young
hand dropped in its little wreath ; many a stifled sob was
heard. Some—and they were not a few—knelt down. All
were sincere and truthful in their sorrow. The service done,
the mourners stood apart, and the villagers closed round to
look into the grave before the stone should be replaced.

One called to mind how he had seen her sitting on that very
spot, and how her book had fallen on her lap, and she was
gazing with a pensive face upon the sky. Another told how
he had wondered much that one so delicate as she should be
so bold ; how she had never feared to enter the church alone
at night, but had loved to linger there when all was quiet,
and even to climb the tower-stair with no more light than
that of the moon-rays stealing through the loopholes in the
thick old walls.

A whisper went about among the oldest there that she had
seen and talked with angels ; and, when they called to mind
how she had looked and spoken, and her early death, some
thought it might be so indeed. Thus coming to the grave
in little knots, and glancing down, and giving place to others,
and falling off in whispering groups of three or four, the

church was cleared in time of all but the sexton and the mourning friends.

Then, when the dusk of evening had come on, and not a sound disturbed the sacred stillness of the place, when the bright moon poured in her light on tomb and monument, on pillar, wall and arch, and most of all, it seemed to them, upon her quiet grave,—in that calm time when all outward things and inward thought teem with assurances of immortality, and worldly hopes and fears are humbled in the dust before them, — then, with tranquil and submissive hearts, they turned away, and left the child with God.—*Dickens.*

CIRCULAR AND TESTIMONIALS.

BRAKIGRAPHY.

The great superiority of Brakigraphy over the old systems of short-hand has been fully demonstrated during the past year, the majority of our own students having learned to write in a six months' course, at a speed varying from 100 to 150 words per minute, and to read their notes at sight.

During the year we obtained situations for twenty-seven students, and between twenty and thirty secured positions for themselves, making in all over fifty who commenced, completed their course, and put their knowledge to practical use within the year. Students of the old systems are forced to acknowledge that such a degree of proficiency cannot be attained by them; and the question naturally suggests itself, whether it would not be wise on their part to drop a system which they can neither write nor read, and take up one in which they can have assurance of success.

A well-known manufacturer of Pittsburgh in a conversation lately, remarked to the author that, having advertised for a stenographer, he had four applicants who used one of the old systems. Three of the applicants had from two to three years' experience, but they were all rejected, because, when called upon, they could not read their own writing. We have no hesitation in saying that not one of the fifty of our students who took situations last year, will ever be discharged for that cause.

For the benefit of those who have been wearing out their brains for years in a vain endeavor to master the arbitrary

signs of the old systems, while our students master Brakigraphy and accept situations in a few months, we publish
letters from some of them, regretting that want of space
obliges us to curtail the number.

It is a note-worthy fact, that writers of Brakigraphy being
able to read their notes at sight, and consequently able to
perform a large amount of work in a day, command much
higher salaries than writers of the old systems, who lose at
least half their time endeavoring to decipher their writing.

SELF-INSTRUCTION.

The " Elements of Brakigraphy" has been prepared espec-
ially to meet the want of those who have not the means to
take a course of instruction under a teacher.

No person of ordinary education and facility with the pen,
need have any fears of failure to learn from this little book,
provided he has energy sufficient to carry through successfully
any ordinary project of life. In this book is embodied the
experience of two years of successful teaching; and the lessons
are presented in precisely the same form as those given by
mail to students at a distance. The student will find that
very little mental labor is required after the first chapter has
been thoroughly mastered; and the rapidity of his progress will
depend for the most part on his application to practice.

Unlike the old arbitrary systems, Brakigraphy is a science,
and the student perceives a reason for every step in his progress;
and as his ability to record the exact words of a speaker
increases, the fascination of the study increases to such an
extent that he is frequently tempted to neglect other duties in
order to devote more time to it.

In order that it may be within reach of all, the price of the
" Elements of Brakigraphy" has been fixed at one dollar,
which, considering the heavy expense of the engraving, is
very low.

PITTSBURGH COLLEGE OF SHORT-HAND.

To those who desire to prepare themselves for the actual business of reporting in the shortest time possible, our school offers superior advantages.

The course of instruction embraces a thorough drill in rapid reading and writing, criticism, the proper forms for captions of legal documents, preparing copy for the printer, punctuation, letter writing, and, in short, everything necessary to fit the stenographer for a successful performance of the duties of any branch of the profession.

Within a few years type-writing has become an almost indispensable adjunct to stenography for the speedy transcription of short-hand notes, and students receive careful instruction therein. Our school is supplied with a number of Remington type-writers, of which students have the use until they become proficient.

We do not guarantee to procure situations for students, but, having many applications for stenographers from business firms, we always fill such situations with our best students.

We have no classes. Each student has a lesson assigned to him individually, the principles of which are fully explained, and, after a thorough oral drill, he is required to take the lesson to his home or room, and practice writing it until the principles are indelibly impressed upon his memory, when he is ready for another lesson.

The charge for the entire course (time unlimited), including instruction on the type-writer, and in everything necessary to make a first-class stenographer, is thirty dollars in advance. This is the cheapest course a student can take, as there are no restrictions to it, the student being at liberty to stop when interrupted with other business, and resume again at pleasure.

For the benefit of those who have not the means to pay for the entire course in advance, we have made a special arrangement, which includes the same instruction as the former, but the student is not at liberty to lose time, unless at his own expense. The charge for instruction in this way is five dollars per month in advance. To students at a distance, a thorough knowledge of short-hand will be given by mail for the same price. Many successful reporters have been made in this way.

The charge for a single lesson is one dollar.

Type-writer instruction without short-hand is five dollars per month in advance. This entitles the student to nine hours practice per week, and careful instruction in the operation and care of the instrument.

Teachers of Brakigraphy supplied with circulars, books, paper, pens, etc., at cost.

EMPLOYMENT AND SALARIES.

Stenographers are extensively employed by the Courts throughout the United States, by Congress and the Legislatures of the different States, by lawyers, clergymen, railroad companies, telegraph companies, express companies, mercantile and manufacturing firms, insurance companies and agencies, commercial agencies—in short, wherever there is much writing to do, and economy of time necessary, stenographers are employed.

Stenographers who use Brakigraphy generally begin on salaries ranging from $40 to $60 per month, and, as they acquire experience, their salaries are increased until they reach $125, or more, per month. Stenographers of experience, who engage in law reporting, make from $3,000 to $6,000 per annum.

We are in constant receipt of letters of inquiry concerning short-hand, and have endeavored to answer them in this circular. Should anyone, however, desire information not already answered, he is cordially invited to call upon or address the author at the Germania Bank Building, Pittsburgh, Pa.

TESTIMONIALS.

From the Pittsburgh Telegraph.

Mr. John T. Porter is the oldest short-hand reporter in Pittsburgh, and has had a very large experience in the Courts. * * * His system of short-hand is unique; by its use a saving of thirty per cent. is effected over the "Graham," which hitherto has been considered the most abbreviated system extant.

From the Pittsburgh Post.

The merits of Brakigraphy are that it is so simple in construction as to be easily understood, easily remembered, and can be written with the rapidity of speech, without extraordinary effort by the short-hand writer.

From the Pittsburgh Sunday Leader.

* * * * * This system of short-band, termed Brakigraphy, has the merit of being so plain and simple that it is easily acquired by any person of ordinary intelligence.

From the Pittsburgh Legal Journal.

Edited by E. Y. BRECK, Official Stenographer of Common Pleas Court No. 1.

Mr. Porter's work will meet the demand for a system of short-hand capable of being used in ordinary business transactions. Being founded upon the vowels, instead of the consonants, as in other systems, it is so legible that stenographers using it can readily read each others notes; and so brief that the author claims it exceeds in speed, by almost one-third, the most rapid of the old systems. Many young men who began the study of the art under Mr. Porter's tutelage a few months ago, are now filling situations as stenographic correspondents in this city and elsewhere.

The author has been long and favorably known as an accomplished stenographer of the Graham and Pitman schools, and the fact that he now writes his own system with greater ease and speed, and increased legibility, is an excellent recommendation of its worth.

Mr. J. T. PORTER, Esq , Dear Sir:—I have made a somewhat critical examination of your system of short-hand writing, called Brakigraphy, and must say that upon a comparison of it with the

6

several systems of Phonography now in general use, I find it is from twenty-five to thirty per cent. shorter; and in the matter of legibility it is superior to any system of short-hand extant.

Your admirable classification of the elementary sounds of the language will undoubtedly divest the study of the art of many of its disagreeable features, one of which is the tediousness incident to committing to memory long lists of arbitrary word-signs.

Very respectfully,

GEO. B. LIPPINCOTT,

Official Stenographer, Common Pleas No. 1, Pittsburgh, Pa.

After a careful examination of Brakigraphy, I am able to say that I believe it surpasses in speed and legibility any of the old systems now in use. It is founded upon an entirely new theory, and answers perfectly the demand of the times for a system of short-hand writing, easy to learn, easy to read, and easily written.

W. A. SCHMIDT,

Court Stenographer, Office 139 Fourth Ave., Pittsburgh, Pa.

After examining the system of Brakigraphy, or phonic short-hand, I find that it is an improvement over the old systems. Mr. Porter has proven conclusively that a system built upon vowels instead of consonants is more easily learned, and that greater speed is acquired. Beginners now in his system have not the difficulties to encounter that we older stenographers had when we began our studies. There have been many improvements in the art of short-hand writing, but all the late system were founded more or less on the earlier efforts of phonographic authors and I congratulate the author of Brakigraphy that he has had the courage to turn aside from the well beaten path.

A. E. LUTY,

Stenographer of the Dispatch, Pittsburgh, Pa.

I might be appropriately denominated a Brakigraphical enthusiast. While studying Brakigraphy I was closely occupied in in a school room during the day, and had only my evenings to devote to practice, and as may be inferred my mind was less bright after teaching all day than it would have been had my occupation been less laborious. After precisely six months' study, I found that I could write 100 words per minute with perfect ease.

Miss CARRIE V. YOUNG,

Stenographer for the "Iron Age," Office 77 Fourth Ave.,

Pittsburgh, Pa.

After studying Brakigraphy for seven months, I was able to write about 100 words per minute on an average, and accepted a position where I am putting it to practical use.

W. J. FLEMING,
Stenographer for the P., C. & St. L. Railway Co.,
Pittsburgh, Pa.

After studying Brakigraphy for about four months, I was able to write about from 75 to 80 words per minute. For rapidity, legibility, and the ease with which it is learned, it is undoubtedly the best system of short-hand now in use.

W. H. STURGEON, Jr.,
Pittsburgh, Pa.

At a very low estimate I could write 100 words per minute after devoting four hours per day for five months to the study of Brakigraphy.

Miss IDA E. BARNES,
Independent Stenographer, Office 136 Fifth Ave.,
Pittsburgh, Pa.

I have studied Brakigraphy, and take pleasure in commending it to all who may have a desire to acquire a knowledge of this useful art.

JAMES H. YOUNG,
Stenographer for Paine, Ablett & Co., Limited

I was at one time a student of Pitman's system of short-hand, but having learned to write Brakigraphy, can truthfully say that I consider it much superior to any system of short hand that I have ever examined. Six months of study and practice have enabled me to put it to practical use in taking depositions, etc. It is speedy, accurate and easily read, and altogether I am delighted with it.

S. C. CLARK,
Attorney at Law, Washington, Pa.

I took lessons in Brakigraphy between six and seven months, devoting about four hours per day to its study and could then write 115 words per minute.

Miss SADIE E. HILDERBRAND,
Stenographer for S. S. Marvin & Co., Liberty St., Pittsburgh, Pa.

I have taken instructions in Brakigraphy from you for about five months, and can now write 120 words per minute, and have no difficulty whatever in reading it. To anyone desiring to reach competency in this profession, your system offers superior advantages in simplicity, legibility and rapidity.

Recommending Brakigraphy to all who desire to become proficient in this beautiful art,

I am, yours very truly,

L. G. GARRETT,

Stenographer for the Pittsburgh Fire Arms Co.

Dear Sir.—It may be interesting to you to know how I am succeeding with Brakigraphy. I have been practicing at home a few months, and can write 130 words per minute, and I entertain the very highest opinion of its merits.

W. B. DUVALL,

Croom Station, Prince George's Co., Maryland.

After having studied Graham's system of short-hand for some time, I was induced to take up Brakigraphy, and have found it much more easily learned. One of its many advantages is the absence of the long lists of arbitrary word-signs found in the old systems.

W. K. McELROY,

Car Accountant Office, Allegheny Valley R. R., Pittsburgh, Pa.

After studying your system of short-hand for about four months, I found that I could write 120 words per minute.

Miss **BERTIE F. CAMPBELL,**

Pittsburgh, Pa.,

Stenographer for Paine, Ablett & Co., Limited.

J. T. Porter, Esq.—Dear Sir:—I believe my fourth month has about expired. * * * I have been sick a great part of the time, and our business has been unusually good this fall, in consequence of which I have been very busy. However, I am able to write about 70 words per minute, and I feel confident that if I could have devoted from two to four hours each day, during the past four months to the study of your system, I could by this time have reached a speed of 100 words per minute. I remain,

Yours very respectfully,

E. H. LEIZURE,

McKeesport, Pa.

I have studied Brakigraphy between five and six months, and can write 135 words per minute. Its simplicity and its ease of comprehension make it a delightful study.

A person's evenings cannot be spent more profitably, nor yet more pleasantly than in its practice.

C. C. SMITH,

Corresponding Stenographer for F. & J. Heinz, Pittsburgh, Pa.

JOHN T. PORTER, Esq.—Dear Sir:—In January last I first thought of learning short-hand, and after a preliminary examination of several systems, I selected yours, as it seemed to me that I could see the principle upon which it was based, which I could not then see (nor do I yet) in the old systems. I feel more than pleased that I did so, as I can now, after six months' study, write any matter from dictation, with a speed of 120 words per minute with ease.

I cheerfully recommend your system as being easily understood, and easily acquired by anyone with application, and as being easily read when acquired.

Very respectfully,

CHARLES M. SOUTH,

Stenographer for the P., F. W. & C. R. R. Co.

Mr South is but fourteen years of age.

I studied Brakigraphy under Mr. Porter's tuition for about six months. On a test I was able to write 150 words per minute. Its simplicity, its one style of writing and its lack of word-signs make it easy to learn.

A. E. B. ANDERSON,

Corresponding 'Stenographer for the Elba Iron and Bolt Co., Limited, Pittsburgh, Pa.

I studied Brakigraphy a little over five months. At the expiration of that time I could write 130 words per minute. As a profession, I think short-hand writing ranks highest among those selected by women and would recommend it to all who yet have a choice to make. Brakigraphy is I think, the best system of shorthand extant, and is at the same time the most scientific, shortest, and easiest to comprehend.

Miss MARY B DAVIS,

Stenographer for Census Bureau, Pittsburgh, Pa.

Having lost my right arm a few years ago, I was tempted to advance my position in life, and took up Porter's system of shorthand, and after taking lessons from Mr. Porter about four months I could write 120 words per minute very nicely. I take pleasure in recommending Brakigraphy to the public as the very best system extant. I am at present employed by the P. R. R. Co.

O. A. HOLLINGSWORTH.

JOHN T. PORTER, Esq.—Dear Sir:—Mr. Walker came in a few minutes since, and, as he often does, began to dictate a letter very rapidly. I had no paper at hand except a blank pad, upon which I took the letter. I enclose the original notes and transcription of same. Can this be done by stenographers of short experience using the old systems ?

I have never had the slightest difficulty in transcribing my notes. although sometimes written with a "stub" pen. I can average over 125 words per minute on general work for any length of time, and took a sermon a few weeks since at an average speed of 138 words a minute; speed reaching at times 166 words a minute, and transcribed same.

Yours truly,

H. C. WEBSTER,

Stenographer for the Union Forge and Iron Co., Limited,

Pittsburgh, Pa.

After studying your system of short-hand about four months, I was able to write about 120 words per minute. I have finished and am filling a pleasant position. I like my work, and think it is certainly the most suitable occupation open to ladies.

Yours respectfully,

Miss BIRDIE WESTERVELT,

Stenographer for Hussey, Binns & Co.

After six months study of your system I am enabled to take down 125 words per minute readily. I heartily recommend it to those desiring to acquire the art in a comparatively short time.

Yours, etc.,

OSCAR L. KLEBER,

122 Wood St., Pittsburgh, Pa.

I take pleasure in testifying to the superiority of your system of stenography. After having studied it but six months I was able to write 120 words per minute of anything, which, I think could not have been accomplished in so short a space of time by studying any of the older systems.

I am respectfully,

KOLLY KLEBER,

122 Wood St, Pittsburgh, Pa.

Having taken personal instruction in Brakigraphy, I find after five months' study and practice, averaging three hours per day, I can at a low estimate write 100 words per minute. I take pleasure in adding my name to your fast filling list of testimonials in a system of short-hand which must shortly be accorded the front rank by all Stenographers—a place to which it is justly entitled.

For speed, legibility, and the ease with which it is acquired, it certainly surpasses all others.

Respectfully yours,

Miss BERTHA E. YOUNG.

PRACTICAL EXERCISES

IN

BRAKIGRAPHY,

BY

JOHN T. PORTER,

PITTSBURGH, PA.

A book supplementing the principles developed in the "Elements of Brakigraphy," with exhaustive practice in actual business reporting, such as deeds, mortgages, articles of agreement, testimony, specifications for buildings and patents, letter writing, etc. To ensure accurate work in any branch of reporting, it is absolutely necessary that the stenographer should have some experience in that branch before undertaking it. The surest and quickest way to gain this experience is by confining his practice to the subject matter of his future work, instead of desultory practice on miscellaneous subjects.

Sent postpaid to any address on receipt of price, $2.00.

GERMANIA BANK BUILDING, PITTSBURGH, PA.